Heroes Don't Just Happen

Biographies of Overcoming Bias and Building Character

in Space

Corinne J. Naden
Rose Blue

The Peoples Publishing Group, Inc.
Free to Learn, to Grow, to Change
1-800-822-1080

Credits

Editor, Charmaine Harris-Stewart
Production/Electronic Design, Kristine Liebman
Cover Design, Westchester Graphic Group
Design, Doreen E. Smith
Photo Research, Kristine Liebman

Photo Credits:

pg. 6, 8, NASA, pg. 11, 12, 13, Special Thanks to Tracey Lawrence, pg. 18, 23, 28, 30, 36, NASA, 39, University of Colorado at Boulder, Alumni Association, 41, 44, 47, NASA, pg. 52 University of Colorado at Boulder, Alumni Association, pg. 57, 59, 65, 67, 68, 73, NASA, pg. 76, 77, Special Thanks to Rosanne Ochoa, pg. 82, 83, 85, NASA

ISBN 1-56256-431-5

The Peoples Publishing Group, Inc.
230 West Passaic Street
Maywood, New Jersey 07607

Printed in the United States of America.

10 9 8 7 6 5 4

To the Student

As you read Heroes Don't Just Happen, you will want to complete the Practice Journal. It gives you practice on vocabulary, reading comprehension, writing, and sequencing and also asks you to write personal, private journal entries of your own. If a teacher is helping you, he or she will check your answers to the vocabulary, comprehension, and sequencing activities and will give you feedback on the writing activity. Your personal journal writing is yours alone. It is private and will not be graded, although your teacher may check to be sure that you are writing personal journal entries. You will notice that, as you progress through this book, your vocabulary will build. You will also notice that the vocabulary will help you understand better what you read in newspapers and magazines. The other skills activities will also help you improve your reading skills.

With your language and writing skills, practice is needed if you want to succeed. It's up to you. But this is only one of the lessons you will learn from reading about Robert H. Lawrence, Jr., Guion S. Bluford, Jr., Ellison S. Onizuka, Mae C. Jemison, and Ellen Ochoa.

You will also be challenged to think hard and to develop your own set of values. You are the only one who can decide what your personal best should be. Begin your practice journal now and work hard. When you finish it, decide how your values have changed. Set new goals for yourself. Don't ever stop. Be the best you can be.

Heroes Don't Just Happen
Biographies of Overcoming Bias and Building Character

IN **SPACE**

Contents

"

Flying was his heart.

"

Robert H. Lawrence, Jr.
1935-1967

ROBERT H. LAWRENCE, JR.

First Selected African American Astronaut

1935-1967

Most of the world was shocked—and perhaps more than a little frightened—by the major news story of October 4, 1957. The Soviet Union had launched into orbit the world's first manufactured satellite. The 184-pound *Sputnik* was now circling and looking down on the Earth. People began to use an old word in a new way. The word was *space*. The launching of *Sputnik* had begun the Space Age.

What followed was more of a "space race" between the Soviet Union and the United States, with the Americans just a step behind. The first U.S. satellite, *Explorer I*, went up on January 31, 1958, more than three months after *Sputnik*. In April 1961, the first human, Russian Yuri Gagarin, went into space. The space race narrowed a little that May when astronaut Alan Shepard became the first American shot into space. But Shepard did not orbit, or circle, the Earth. The first American to do that was John Glenn in February 1962. In 1963, the Soviets were first again—cosmonaut Valentina Tereshkova became the world's first woman in space. Tereshkova's flight aboard the *Vostok 6* came 20 years before the first American female astronaut, Sally Ride, blasted off in a space shuttle in April 1983.

Major Robert H. Lawrence, Jr. the first African American to be selected as an astronaut, died before he could realize his dream of traveling in space. His efforts paved the way for other African Americans to travel in space.

So it went in those early years. Then, in July 1969, the United States took a giant space leap forward—U.S. astronaut Neil Armstrong was the first person to step onto the surface of the moon. The *Apollo* had landed, and the space race was never quite the same again. Following the moon landing, increased cooperation between the two countries closed the gap. Later, the breakup of the Soviet Union ended the space race and turned attention more to science. Space launchings became almost commonplace. Unmanned satellites streaked by Mars and Venus and passed near the ringed planet of Saturn. Five, six, and more American astronaut teams blasted off in the space shuttle for several days of orbiting the Earth and performing experiments. These teams increasingly included women and minorities.

The triumphs and defeats that marked the early years of the space program would not be possible without the heroes who knowingly risked danger to advance science. These thoughts were probably not the uppermost thoughts in Major Robert Lawrence's mind on December 8, 1967, as his F-104 Starfighter streaked through the afternoon sky. The sleek jet carried two men. One was Air Force Major Harvey J. Royer, chief of operations for the Aerospace Research Pilot School. Major Robert Henry Lawrence, Jr., the first African American to be selected as an astronaut, was the other.

Six months earlier, Lawrence had completed air force astronaut training. Part of the training involved the F-104 Starfighter. This jet plane can fly at more than 2,254 kilometers an hour and is sometimes called "a missile with a man in it." But something went wrong as the Starfighter headed in to Edwards Air Force Base in California on that early December afternoon. The jet crashed on the runway. When Royer ejected, his safety chute opened. Although he was injured, he survived. But when Lawrence attempted to eject from the rear seat,

Virgil "Gus" Grissom was the second U.S. astronaut to travel in space, which he died on July 21, 1961. He was one of the original seven astronauts selected for the U.S. space program in 1959. Grissom died in flash fire that swept through his space capsule during training on February 21, 1967.

his chute did not open, and he died.

Lawrence became the ninth astronaut to die in an accident and the fifth to die in an air crash. Eleven months earlier, three astronauts—Grissom, Chaffee, and White—died instantly when the capsule in which they were training for a space flight caught fire with them inside during training at the Kennedy Space Center in Florida.

Lawrence's death was a tragic end to a brilliant career. Sixteen years would pass before another African American, Guy Bluford, blazed his way into space.

Robert Lawrence was born on October 2, 1935, 32 years before the fatal crash, in Chicago, Illinois. His family included Robert Sr., mother Gwendalyn, and older sister Barbara. Lawrence's parents divorced when he was very young. He was raised by his mother and his stepfather, Charles Duncan. But they, too, divorced after the children were grown.

The family was poor but close and loving. Duncan, who worked as an underwriter for the Veterans Administration, said that all the family "loved Robert dearly." Robert's mother Gwendalyn, who spent most of her working life as a civil servant, says she can't remember ever having to discipline her son or her

Robert H. Lawrence, Jr. 16, makes a Christmas wish under the loving gaze of his mother, Gwendalyn.

daughter. Today, daughter Barbara is on the staff of the National Scholarship Service and Fund for Negro Students.

Scholarly and serious from his early years, Robert grew up loving model airplanes and chess. He also played the piano, which the family purchased on an installment plan. The deal included some free lessons.

His mother tried to impress upon him the importance of not missing those lessons because money was scarce. Perhaps she made too much of an impression. Runnin through the city streets one afternoon, the boy was hit and knocked down by a truck. He jumped up unhurt and wouldn't allow the driver to take him to the hospital to be checked for fear he'd miss his lesson. Lawrence

Robert H. Lawrence Jr., was an accomplished pianist who mastered the works of several classical composers.

became quite outstanding at the piano. In time, he mastered the works of such classical composers as Rachmaninoff.

Even though Lawrence Jr. was so disciplined, his natural father, a disabled veteran, never thought of him as brilliant. What Lawrence's father saw was a typical eight-year-old boy who played pranks and whose friends called him "Bobjunior" all in one breath.

But it wasn't long before Lawrence's interest in science began to surface and set him apart from his classmates at Haines Elementary School. Each Christmas, Lawrence would ask for a bigger and better chemistry set. At age 12, just around the time he entered Englewood High School, Lawrence developed a passion for biology.

Today, Englewood High, in Chicago's Woodlawn section, suffers all the problems of urban schools throughout the United States. But in the late 1940s, when Lawrence's parents attended Englewood, it was considered a kind of "private public school." It was a place to nurture dreams of a career in science or even space. The families in the mostly African American neighborhood had dreams of their own, spurred on by the prosperity following World War II. They had an interest in keeping standards high and dreams strong at Englewood. For families like the Lawrences who no longer lived in the neighborhood, there were ways to bypass their own area schools and have their children enrolled in Englewood.

Lawrence graduated at age 16 in the top 10 percent of his class. Today, the Robert Lawrence Memorial Library at Englewood marks his memory and his achievements. But he was far from the only achiever. For years afterward, he would sometimes meet with his high school buddies—chemists, engineers, educators, and business and government executives. Among the well-known Englewood grad-uates are playwright Lorraine Hansberry (*A Raisin in the Sun*); former U.S. Secretary of the Interior (1933-1946) Harold Ickes; and lawyer, educator, and ambassador Patricia Harris.

A scholarly and serious Robert H. Lawrence Jr., poses for a class picture.

From Englewood, Lawrence entered Bradley University in

Peoria, Illinois. He joined the Air Force Reserve Officer's Training Corps (ROTC) there. Lawrence rose through the ranks to lieutenant colonel, the school's second-highest-ranking cadet. Former Bradley basketball star Curley Johnson was in his platoon. Johnson remembers Lawrence as "brilliant, very conscientious, military minded, and *very*, *very* strict."

When he graduated in 1956 with a degree in chemistry, Lawrence was made a second lieutenant in the U.S. Air Force. He went on to basic and then advanced flight training, having found his mission in life. As Lawrence Sr. later said, "Flying was his heart."

Flying apparently did not have his entire heart. Part of it was with Barbara Cress, also of Chicago, whom he had met at Bradley. When she earned her degree in psychology in 1958, her father asked her what she wanted for a graduation present. "A trip to Germany," Barbara replied. At the time, Lt. Lawrence was an instructor pilot stationed in Germany. They were married there on July 1, 1958. The couple spent two years in Germany. During that time, they had a son, Tracey.

Lawrence and his young family returned to the United States in 1961. Through the Air Force Institute of Technology, he enrolled at Ohio State University to pursue an advanced degree. Four years later, he earned a doctoral degree in physical chemistry. Lawrence wrote that his work was dedicated to African Americans who spend their lives doing menial work, just trying to

Chicago-born Lorraine Hansberry (1930-1965) became the first African American woman to have a play produced on Broadway when *A Raisin in the Sun* opened in 1959. The play, which featured a working-class African American family in Chicago, won the New York Drama Critics' Circle Award. The film version won an award at Cannes, France, in 1961.

overcome problems of survival. Perhaps, he said, such people think of scientific investigation as a waste of time. He assured them that their own struggles had given him the courage to make the effort to succeed. Lawrence hoped that his success and the way he conducted himself would help to break down some of the social barriers that were tearing the United States apart. Lawrence wrote those words during the difficult years of the Civil Rights struggle in the United States, during the 1960s.

Lawrence decided to take his love of science and flying one step further. When he heard that the National Aeronautics and Space Administration (NASA) was actively seeking recruits for space training, he applied. Twice. Despite his obvious qualifications, he was turned down. Twice. It looked as though NASA wasn't quite ready to change its three-qualification recruitment policy: military jet pilot, male, and white. However, there were some signs of future change. A few years earlier, Edward J. Dwight, Jr., an Air Force captain and jet pilot, received a letter from then President John F. Kennedy. The president had invited Dwight to join the newly established NASA with the aim of becoming the first African American astronaut. Kennedy's assassination in late 1963 ended the plan. Shortly after Kennedy's death, Dwight was transferred to Germany. He was never officially told that he was no longer in the space program. It just wasn't mentioned anymore.

Although turned down by NASA, Lawrence was still determined to pursue his dream. He applied to the Air Force Aerospace Research Pilot School and was accepted for the Manned Orbiting Laboratory program, known as MOL. This was the U.S. military's manned space program, not part of NASA. Lawrence was now in line to become the first African American astronaut. The press made considerable fuss over him. Lawrence, who is normally serious and shy, was uncomfortable with the role. He tried to say that it was all good luck and timing: "I think perhaps I've been a lot more fortunate than many in that several of the people who are responsible for my training just happened to be at the right place at the right time and supplied me with the necessary motivation and the background that I needed."

Lawrence, along with three other air force officers, brought the program-member total to 16 "aerospace research pilots," which is what the air force called these astronauts in 1967. The 16 men were chosen from the 500 military pilots who applied. Women were not allowed in the program at this time.

MOL was not a new idea. The Department of Defense had been entertaining the idea since 1963. At first, MOL was designed just to see how useful—in a military sense a man could be in space. But soon the goals became more ambitious. By 1967, they included three specific goals. The first goal was to learn about what a person could actually do in space and how that ability could be used for U.S. defense. The second goal was to develop both technology and equipment to promote manned and unmanned future space flights. The final specific goal was to experiment with the developed technology and equipment.

To reach these goals, MOL was to be launched in 1970. The 16 astronauts would take turns orbiting or circling the Earth in teams of two for one month. Their mission was to perform experiments, test equipment and technology, and survey the Earth from space.

Lawrence was in his last weeks of training prior to going into space when his Starfighter crashed on December 8, 1967. The air force promised a full investigation but gave very few details of the accident. The press learned that Lawrence and Major Harvey J. Royer were trying to simulate a "lifting body" landing when the tragedy occurred. A lifting body is a wingless craft that was under development at the time. It was intended to return from orbit, reenter the Earth's atmosphere, and land like a conventional aircraft. Practicing such a maneuver is very tricky because it requires a high, abrupt landing and fast touchdown. Instead, the Starfighter smashed into the runway at Edwards Air Force Base.

On June 10, 1969, 18 months after the accident that killed Lawrence, the Department of Defense canceled the MOL program. Some of the air force astronauts

Air force Major Robert H. Lawrence, Jr., shown above with an air force jet, was in his last weeks of training when his aircraft crashed on December 8, 1967, onto a runway at Edwards Air Force Base.

transferred to NASA, which is now the only U.S. agency in the space business.

There were some grumblings after the months-long air force investigation. Why did one parachute open and not the other? The Lawrence family still feels that many questions have not been answered.

Lorne Cress-Love, Lawrence's sister-in-law, describes him as "a wonderful, caring person. He was brilliant but not overly impressed with himself. If you had met him out of uniform, you would never have known that he was a brilliant astronaut, pilot, track star, and piano player. He enjoyed people. He was fun loving and never overbearing. He enjoyed life. Everyone who knew him liked him. He was also very concerned about the young people who sought him out after he was named to the astronaut program. He was always in touch with the children in his old elementary school. He respected the struggle of African Americans who went before him, and he hoped that his work would pave the way for those who came after him."

About his death, Lorne Cress-Love said, "I feel the stress of his loss, and the way he died has still never been settled. Enough inquiry was not made. It was strange. He was not the pilot. His equipment didn't work. Why?"

Barbara Lawrence, who returned to Chicago after her husband's death to raise their eight-year-old son, Tracey, has doubts about her husband's death, too. She remembers that at the time, there were many in the service and government who did not want to see an African American in space. In fact, she said that in the days after Lawrence died, she received many letters of sympathy, as well as a few notes saying that the writer was happy that the accident had happened.

Air Force Major Robert H. Lawrence, Jr., was given a military funeral. White-gloved air force bearers carried his coffin into the First Unitarian Church in Chicago on December 12. Memorial services were also held at Edwards Air Force Base. His family later established the Robert H. Lawrence, Jr., Memorial Scholarship Fund for African American chemistry students at Bradley University.

Lawrence never wanted to be a role model. He just wanted to do his job and fulfill his dream. Nevertheless, he became a role model. His character, his brilliance, and his actions made him one, and reluctant or not, he took the job seriously. How seriously can be seen in his reply to a letter from a third-grade class in Chicago.

"Dear Boys and Girls,

As you become older, you will find that an understanding of the world and its people is very important. A good education will help you to obtain this understanding. Be prepared to take advantage of the wondrous things in the future."

Astronaut Lawrence paid the ultimate price for his personal dream of going into space. Yet, because of his intelligence, hard work, and determination, he and Edward Dwight helped to make the similar dreams of other African Americans a reality. A few years after his death, an editorial appeared in the *Los Angeles Times*, March 21, 1974. It was written by Professor J.K. Obatala, at California State University, Long Beach. Under the headline, "We Need to Correct a Space Age Injustice," Obatala wrote:

> "Now the drama and excitement have ebbed, but the space program is here to stay—indeed, in the years ahead, it will grow rather than diminish in significance. Mars and the moon are as much a part of America's future as are Madison Ave., Hollywood Blvd., and the Mississippi Delta.
>
> From now on, it is essential that the standard of social equality is carried aloft whenever—and wherever—Americans explore. Then the thwarted efforts of Edward Dwight and Robert Lawrence would be redeemed."

* * *

Robert H. Lawrence, Jr.

Career Highlights

1956 Graduates Bradley University, BS in chemistry; begins air force pilot training

1957 Serves as a pilot instructor in West Germany

1961 Enters Ohio State University

1965 Graduates Ohio State, Ph.D. in physical chemistry

1967 Becomes first African American astronaut in Air Force Aerospace Research Pilot School; dies in crash of F-104 Starfighter on December 18, Edwards Air Force Base, CA

Astronaut and role model
Guion S. Bluford, Jr.,
born 1942, says,

"Opportunities do exist for black youngsters if they work hard and strive to take advantage of those opportunities."

GUION S. BLUFORD, JR.

First African American in Space

born 1942

Shortly before Guy Bluford soared into space in late 1983, he visited a high school in Camden, New Jersey. The students, mostly African Americans, had built an experiment to be carried aboard the space shuttle *Challenger*. Bluford began his talk to them by saying, "I'm an engineer and I'm black and I'm lonely out there."

This was astronaut Bluford's way of encouraging minority students to consider a career in science—and space in particular. There were so few African Americans in science and related fields and even fewer in space. That is still true, but increasingly, young minority students are showing an interest in this field. As Bluford well knows, the more students who show an early interest, the greater will be the increase in minority astronauts in the space program.

Guion (Guy) Stewart Bluford, Jr., was born on November 22, 1942, in Philadelphia. He is the oldest of three sons born to Guion, Sr., a mechanical engineer, and Lolita Brice Bluford, a special education teacher. Although everyone calls him "Guy" today, his family used to call him "Bunny."

Hard work, personal achievement, and success were high on the list of goals in the Bluford family. Today, brother Eugene is a hospital x-ray technician in Los Angeles, and brother Kenneth teaches school in Philadelphia.

Ken, who is seven years younger than Guy, says that his brother was "bossy." Bossy or not, everyone who knew him then agreed that he was a quiet child. Guy grew up in a racially mixed, middle-class neighborhood. He worked a paper route, built model airplanes, and reached the rank of Eagle in the Boy Scouts. Today, Bluford says that racial barriers were not a part of his growing-up years. "I thought I could achieve anything I wanted," he said in an interview, "and I just marched on to do it."

It wasn't quite that easy, however. His father's problems began when Guy was about nine years old. Guion Sr. developed epilepsy and mental illness. He died in 1967. "It was rough having an ill father," Guy admits. "Dad was in and out of hospitals and there was always uncertainty." He credits his mother, who died in 1978, with trying hard to keep family life as normal as possible.

Brother Ken remembers little of his father's illness but says, "It was rougher on Guy because he was old enough to understand."

Despite the illness, Guy feels that his father sparked his early interest in math and science. "Dad very much enjoyed being an engineer and worked as much as he could." Guy also became hooked on aviation while attending Hanna Elementary School, which is now renamed in his honor. By the time he entered Overbrook High School, he had decided to become an aerospace engineer.

"I never assumed I would not be able to achieve my goal. I decided to be an aerospace engineer, and I knew I could do it if I planned it right."

Guy may have believed in himself, but his high school counselor wasn't so sure. The counselor told the family that their oldest son might be better off taking up a trade because he wasn't college material. Actually, even his mother felt that Guy was the least likely of the three boys to succeed. He was certainly intelligent and curious, but schoolwork just didn't come easy. Ken remembers that his brother had to work harder than the rest of them to get good grades.

> In 1908, British Cavalry officer Robert S. S. Baden-Powell founded an organization for boys, ages 11 through 15, to teach good citizenship and behavior, as well as outdoor skills. In 1910, the organization became the Boy Scouts of America. Today, there are boy scout troops all over the world. In the United States, the highest award a scout can receive is the Eagle Scout Badge.

However, it was unthinkable that one of the Bluford boys wouldn't go to college. So Guy kept working and studying hard. He also made time to participate in extra activities at his high school. He was captain of the chess team, a member of the science club, and worked on the school yearbook. When he graduated in 1960, he enrolled in the aerospace engineering program at Pennsylvania State University. He was the only African American in that field.

Although Bluford remained quiet and serious, he was obviously a late-blooming student. He became a distinguished cadet in the Air Force Reserve Officer's Training Corps (ROTC), won a Phi Delta Kappa leadership award, and graduated in 1964 with a degree in aerospace engineering. But this was just the start of the dream.

At Penn State, Bluford met and married Linda Tull, also of Philadelphia. They have two sons, Guion III, born in 1964, and James Trevor, born in 1965.

After graduation, Bluford headed for Williams Air Force Base in Arizona, where he received his pilot's wings in January 1965. From there, it was more training in Arizona and Florida and, finally, duty with the 557th Tactical Fighter Squadron in Vietnam. Bluford flew a total of 144 missions, 65 of them over enemy territory in North Vietnam.

Guy was very serious about his work and his sense of duty. Brother Ken, in college during Guy's tour in Vietnam, was, like many young Americans of that period, against the war. But when he tried to talk about it with his brother, Ken says the conversation lasted about 3 minutes. All Guy would say was, "You don't know what you're talking about."

For the next several years after Vietnam, Bluford was kept busy with air force and classroom duties. He was an instructor pilot and assistant flight commander at

Sheppard Air Force Base in Texas. In 1972, he entered the Air Force Institute of Technology, Wright-Patterson Air Force Base in Ohio. This is the leading air force engineering school in the United States.

By 1978, Bluford had earned a doctorate in aerospace engineering, with a minor in laser physics. In January of that year, the National Aeronautics and Space Administration (NASA) chose Bluford, by then an air force lieutenant colonel, as one of 35 candidates to fly in space. These 35 would-be astronauts were chosen from a field of 10,000 applicants. Included in the select few were Sally Ride, who would become the first U.S. woman in space, and two other African Americans, Ronald McNair and Fred Gregory. Tragically, Ron McNair would lose his life on his first ride into space in 1986 when the space shuttle *Challenger* blew up and fell out of the sky after just 73 seconds. Ironically, Bluford's first space trip was also on the *Challenger*, three years earlier.

Between the selection of 35 astronauts in 1978 and Bluford's first flight in 1983, there was much talk about who would be the first African American in space. The United States would probably already have had its first African American astronaut, but Robert Lawrence, in space training years earlier, was killed in 1967. That left four African Americans as possible "firsts:" Bluford, McNair, Gregory, and Lt. Col. Charles F. Bolden, Jr. All four men were selected for the program in 1978.

For Dr. Curtis M. Graves, then a deputy directory at

Astronaut Guy Bluford (left) prepares to perform a physics experiment aboard the space shuttle *Challenger*. He never doubted his ability to achieve a career in space.

NASA, the choice seemed simple. He said, "If I had to invent the first black astronaut, he would be Guy Bluford. . .. He is extraordinarily bright, dedicated, and possesses strong values. As a role model, you couldn't ask for a better person."

The role model himself wasn't so sure. Bluford, who is 6 feet 2 inches tall and weighs 180 pounds, describes himself merely as a "quietish person who loves airplanes." He wasn't wild about a possible role in the limelight. "It might be better," he said, "to be second or third because then you can enjoy it and disappear—return to the society you came out of without someone always poking you in the side and saying you were first."

But no such luck. The "quietish" person with the passion for flying was destined to make history.

In the meantime, Bluford and his family settled in Houston, Texas, where he began his training at the Lyndon B. Johnson Space Center. Somewhat to his surprise, Bluford found that he enjoyed the rigors of training. "It gives me a chance to use all my skills and do something that is pretty exciting. The job is so fantastic that you don't need a hobby. The hobby is going to work."

"Work" included courses in oceanography, space navigation, geology, and celestial mechanics. He learned to parasail off the Florida coast, to land on water as well as on land, and to survive for days at sea in an open raft. He studied the thousand-and-one things an astronaut needs to know to survive in the foreign element known as space.

After a year of these basic studies, Bluford entered advanced training for the specific mission he would fly. Now he was eligible for selection as a mission specialist on a space-shuttle flight. It would be his responsibility to coordinate activities that related to scientific and engineering experiments on the mission.

Five years of hard work and training passed by. Then NASA made its decision. The flight of the space shuttle *Challenger* scheduled for August or September 1983 would be manned by five astronauts: commander Dick Truly, pilot Dan Brandenstein, and mission specialists William Thorton, Dale Gardner, and Guion Stewart

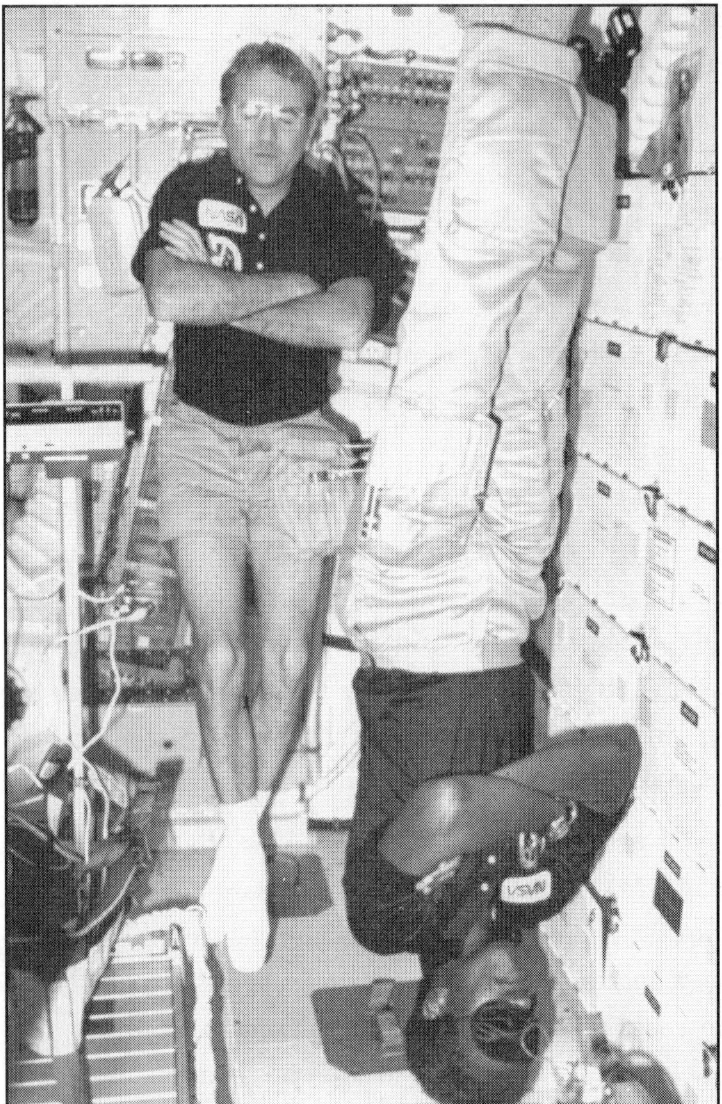

At right, mission specialist Guy Bluford's space work includes learning how to relax and let his body float upside down during a rest session onboard the space capsule.

Bluford, Jr. Whether he wanted the role or not, Guy Bluford was to become the first African American in space.

When he heard the news, Bluford acted in his usual low-key fashion. He finished some paperwork at his desk before he went home to tell his wife, then an accountant with an oil firm, and his teenage sons.

Bluford's selection placed him in the company of other pioneers in space. Among the other "firsts" in the U.S. astronaut program was Sally Ride. Ride became the "first" woman U.S. astronaut on the flight before Bluford's. Outside the United States, Bluford, although the first African American in space, was not the first black astronaut in space. In 1980, Arnaldo Tamayo Mendez, a Cuban, had been on the Soviet Union's *Soyuz 38* space flight.

Today, Guy Bluford says that his greatest sense of achievement came from the actual flight itself, not because he was the first African American astronaut. The mission itself was remarkable in its own right. It was slated to be the first night launch of a shuttle in U.S. space history. The night flight was necessary to place a weather and communications satellite in proper orbit, which was one of Bluford's main responsibilities. The *Challenger* would also be carrying the oldest U.S. astronaut—Dr. William Thorton, age 54.

The *Challenger* mission was scheduled for takeoff on August 30, 1983. In the prelaunch hours, lightning and rain covered the launch pad at the Kennedy Space Center in Florida. As Bluford and the rest of the crew, in space gear and helmets, waited for a break in the weather, a large crowd gathered. They braved the elements to see the first night launch and the first African American astronaut make history. In the crowd were government officials and such well-known personalities as jazz musician Lionel Hampton and comedian Bill Cosby.

But Bluford was mostly focusing on the weather. The launch was on again, off again. It looked good. It looked doubtful. Then, as the countdown reached T minus 9, meaning 9 minutes until launch, the rain stopped. At exactly 2:32 A.M., launch pad 39-A erupted in an enormous, brilliant orange ball. The onlookers were stunned into silence as the 100-ton spaceship *Challenger* shook the earth and screamed into the sky in a breathtaking plume of noise, smoke, and fire. The spectacular fireworks could be seen as far away as Miami, 323 kilometers (about 200 miles) to the north.

The shuttle crew was also impressed. Pilot Brandenstein said that the liftoff made him feel as though he was "inside a bonfire." Mission specialist Gardner looked back at the sight and thought for a moment that he had blinded himself. Mission specialist Bluford was more impressed by his experience in orbit than he was with the takeoff. "The ride up . . . wasn't as exhilarating as most people think," he said later. "People tend to think that you're thrown back in your seat when you lift off. No . . . it was a smooth, gentle ride up. The experience of orbit was fantastic. . . ."

"Fantastic" pretty much described the entire six-day mission. On the second day, Bluford successfully launched the communications satellite for the government of India. Along with Gardner, he also guided the space shuttle's 15.24-meter (50-foot) mechanical arm to test how to retrieve and deploy malfunctioning satellites in space. He conducted experiments with human, dog, and rat cells, as well as an experiment known as *electrophoresis*. Electrophoresis is an electronic process that aids in the fight against diabetes and heart disease.

The mission was a great success. President Ronald Reagan called the *Challenger* crew in space and especially noted Bluford. "Guy," said the president, "you, I think, are paving the way for many others, and you are making it plain that we are in an era of brotherhood here in our land, and you will serve as a role model for so many others. . . ."

When the *Challenger* landed in the Mojave Desert, California, at 3:40 A.M. on September 5, coming home was almost as awesome as taking off. After 98 orbits of the Earth, the space shuttle swooped down out of the early morning sky. It glided along a desert runway lit by 4.8 billion candlepower, the world's most powerful floodlights. Bluford told the waiting crowd and the press, "I'm really humbled tonight to see so many people out here. . . . I feel very proud to be a member of this team, and I think we have a tremendous future with the space shuttle—I mean *all* of us."

An orbit is the path of a body or mass circling another, like a spaceship around the Earth or the Earth around the sun. Scientists Johannes Kepler and Isaac Newton discovered the physical laws governing orbits back in the seventeenth century.

Bluford's Aunt Lucille was in the welcoming home crowd. A native of Kansas City where she still lives and once edited a newspaper, a proud Aunt Lucille told her nephew that the town had declared Guion Bluford Day in his honor.

The "first" mission was over but not Bluford's space career. On October 30, 1985, he was part of the crew aboard the German *D-1 Spacelab*, launched from Kennedy Space Center in Florida. It carried eight astronauts, and the shuttle's largest crew and completed 111 Earth orbits.

This was Bluford's last flight in space for nearly six years. NASA shut down its shuttle missions for more than two years following the January 1986 *Challenger* explosion that killed all seven crew members aboard. Bluford's third flight, aboard the *Discovery*, didn't take place until April 28, 1991. The mission returned to Earth after 134 orbits.

The astronaut's fourth and last mission for NASA blasted off on December 2, 1991. Bluford was part of the five-member crew that was responsible for setting up a classified payload—the material and equipment carried into space—for the Department of Defense. The mission returned seven days later, having completed 115 Earth orbits. At his return, Bluford had spent more than 688 hours in space.

Guion S. Bluford, Jr., the quiet man witha passion

for flying, retired from NASA in 1993. As a role model for young people, especially young African Americans, and as a role model for aspiring pilots and astronauts, he served well. Because of the work and character of Bluford and other early pioneers, minority groups are far better represented in the space program today.

The Egyptians used candles as far back as 3000 B.C. *Candlepower*, or the measurement of how intense candlelight is, was defined as one-sixth of a pound of sperm wax burning at 120 grains per hour. Today candles are used mainly as decorations, but they're still handy when the electricity goes out!

Bluford became general manager of the Engineering Service Division of NYMA, a Maryland-based company that sells computer software to NASA. Today, he is vice president and general manager of an NYMA branch in Brook Park, Ohio. Bluford's branch provides engineering services to NASA. He and his wife live in nearby Olmsted. Their sons are out of college and no longer live at home.

Although Guy Bluford still avoids the spotlight, he tries to live up to his status as a role model. He is often a speaker at schools and is an active alumna for Penn State. "Guy talks to students about NASA, engineering, and such. He comes back often," says Andrea Messer, the university's media director.

In his talks to students, Bluford stresses the need to pursue science and engineering and a career in space. "From a black perspective," he said, "my flight on the shuttle was important because it represented another step forward. . . . Opportunities do exist for black

Bluford, on his third mission, poses with crew aboard the space shuttle *Discovery*. Left to right (front) are astronauts Donald R. McMonagle; Michael L. Coats; Charles L. (Lacy) Veach, and Gregory J. Harbaugh. Left to right (rear) are astronauts Guion S. Bluford, Jr., L. Blaine Hammond, and Richard J. Hieb.

youngsters if they work hard and strive to take advantage of those opportunities."

Guy Bluford took advantage, and it took him right out of this world.

***

Guion S. Bluford, Jr.

Career Highlights

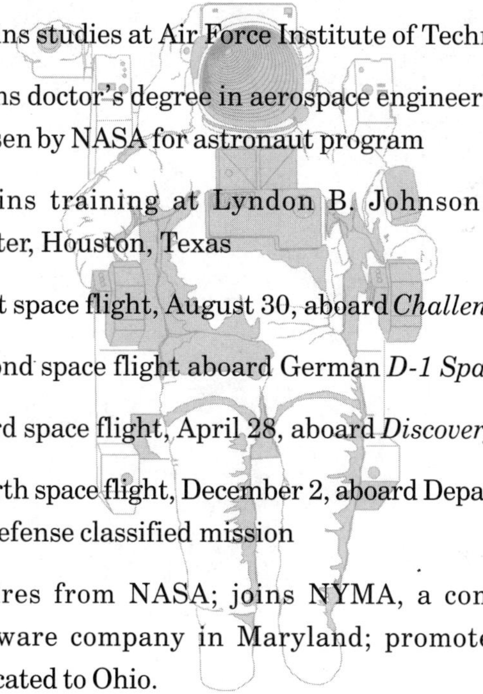

1965 Earns pilot's wings, Williams Air Force Base; tour of duty in Vietnam

1972 Begins studies at Air Force Institute of Technology

1978 Earns doctor's degree in aerospace engineering; chosen by NASA for astronaut program

1979 Begins training at Lyndon B. Johnson Space Center, Houston, Texas

1983 First space flight, August 30, aboard *Challenger*

1985 Second space flight aboard German *D-1 Spacelab*

1991 Third space flight, April 28, aboard *Discovery*

1991 Fourth space flight, December 2, aboard Department of Defense classified mission

1993 Retires from NASA; joins NYMA, a computer software company in Maryland; promoted and relocated to Ohio.

"

If you can't do it well, don't do it at all.

"

Ellison S. Onizuka

1946-1986

ELLISON S. ONIZUKA

First Japanese American In Space

1946-1986

It might look terrifying to watch someone being hurtled into space in a bright orange cloud and a roar that could break an eardrum, but it worked every time . . . until that fateful day, January 28, 1986. Seventy-three seconds into its flight and about 15,300 meters (50,000 feet) in the sky, the space shuttle *Challenger* blew up. It sent all seven U.S. astronauts aboard to a quick and fiery death. Among the seven was the first Japanese American in space. He was 39-year-old, Hawaiian-born Ellison S. Onizuka. The *Challenger* was his second shuttle flight.

El, as his friends called him, was warm, fun loving, and determined. "I still have to pinch myself to convince me that the dream came true," he said after being selected for astronaut training in 1978.

Ellison Shoji Onizuka was born in Kealakekua, Hawaii, on June 14, 1946. He grew up in the farming community of Keopu, in the shadow of Kilauea Iki, the world's most active volcano. This is part of the lush tropical paradise known as the Kona Coast. The vegetation, however, was the only thing lush abut El's childhood. His parents, Masamitsu and Mitsue, ran a tiny store that sold general merchandise. Onizuka's

Always funloving, Onizuka plays a prank with "kamakaze" headband on fellow crewmember Loren J. Shriver, asleep aboard the space shuttle *Discovery*.

grandparents on his father's side were farmers who had emigrated from Japan in the late 1800s.

There were four children in the Onizuka family: Shirley, Norma, Ellison, and Claude. Their parents told them that if they wanted to get ahead, they had better work for it. Ellison helped out at the store and on his grandfather's coffee farm. When he wasn't working, Ellison liked to cut paper airplanes from old catalogs. He often predicted, "I'm going to drive a plane when I grow up."

In Honokobau Elementary School, Onizuka was a bright, inquisitive, somewhat shy, but friendly boy. Through his school years, he learned his lessons quickly, and he also found time for Little League, and the 4-H Club and to become an Eagle Scout. Usually, it takes six years to make Eagle Scout, but Onizuka did it in four. He was determined and methodical. If he set out to do something, he made a plan for his goal and then did it.

Onizuka, who grew to a height of 5 feet 9 inches and 162 pounds, played on the Konawaena High School basketball and baseball teams. Although he did not have great physical talent, he made up for it in hard work and spirit. He was also the president of the Hawaii 4-H Club Federation. His friends remember him as friendly and fun loving but determined and a dreamer, too.

His dream was still to "drive an airplane." When his school friends discussed possible future careers, Onizuka already knew his. In 1962, Wally Schirra, one of America's first seven astronauts, splashed down near Hawaii after a successful ride in space. From that time on, young Ellison was not only hooked on airplanes but on space as well. He announced to his family that he would become an astronaut. His grandfather laughed at his dreamer grandson.

The grandson, however, did what he always did. He made plans. The next step to achieving his dream was to become an aerospace engineer. But no university in Hawaii offered such a program. So, after high school graduation in 1964, Onizuka traveled 1,610 meters (1,000 miles) to follow his dream at the University of Colorado in Boulder. He had been awarded a Reserve Officers Training Corps (ROTC) scholarship.

Onizuka had made the first step toward his childhood dream, but he didn't forget his old friends. Soon after his arrival in Colorado, he wrote a letter to his Eagle

Scout leader. He said that his heart would always be with the boys back home. "Once an Eagle, always an Eagle," he said.

Onizuka was popular with his college classmates. One professor remembered him as personable, positive, and enthusiastic. During his college years, Onizuka was a member of the engineering club and student government and was listed in *Who's Who in American Universities and Colleges*. However, an otherwise wonderful first year was marred by his father's death from a heart attack. A sad Onizuka returned to Hawaii for the funeral.

By December 1969, Onizuka had earned both bachelor and master of science degrees in aerospace engineering. There were other changes in his life as well. At the university, he met Lorna Leiko Yoshida of Pahala, Hawaii, who was studying to become a teacher. They were married soon after Onizuka earned his degrees. The couple had two daughters, Janelle Mitsue, born in 1969, and Darien Lei Shizue, born in 1975. Lorna Onizuka remembers her husband as a caring and helpful father. Janelle was so tiny as an infant that Lorna was afraid to pick her up, so Onizuka often was the parent who took care of her.

Onizuka was now a husband, a father, and an aerospace engineer. He had completed the first leg of his career. But what about space? How could he get there?

After four years in the ROTC program, Onizuka began active duty as a second lieutenant with the U.S. Air Force in January 1970. His first tour was at McClellen Air

Force Base, Sacramento, California. He conducted flight test programs and systems safety engineering for various jet aircraft.

Onizuka was born on the largest of the 20 Hawaiian Islands, the island of Hawaii. The islands themselves are the actual tops of volcanic and coral islands in the Pacific Ocean. Two volcanoes—Mauna Loa and Kilauea—are active. With a little more than 15,540 square kilometers (6,000 square miles), Hawaii ranks 43rd of the 50 states in land area. Its capital is Honolulu on the island of Oahu. Hawaii became the 50th state on August 21, 1959.

McClellen was a challenging duty tour, but it wasn't space. It wasn't even leading to space. So Onizuka applied to the United States Air Force Test Pilot School at Edwards Air Force Base in California. He felt that test pilot experience would give him good experience as a possible candidate for the astronaut program.

Onizuka put his dream to become an astronaut on hold during his time at Edwards. He logged more than 1,700 hours of flying time between August 1974 and July 1975. He also worked as a flight-test engineer and received instruction in all types of jet aircraft.

Onizuka remained at Edwards for three more years as an instructor. The atmosphere was very competitive because most of the officers there wanted to make the space program as much as Onizuka did. His hours were long and hard. What was left of his precious free time was spent coaching the Little League team at the base. All this, of course, left less time for his family. Lorna Onizuka does not remember this period as being their

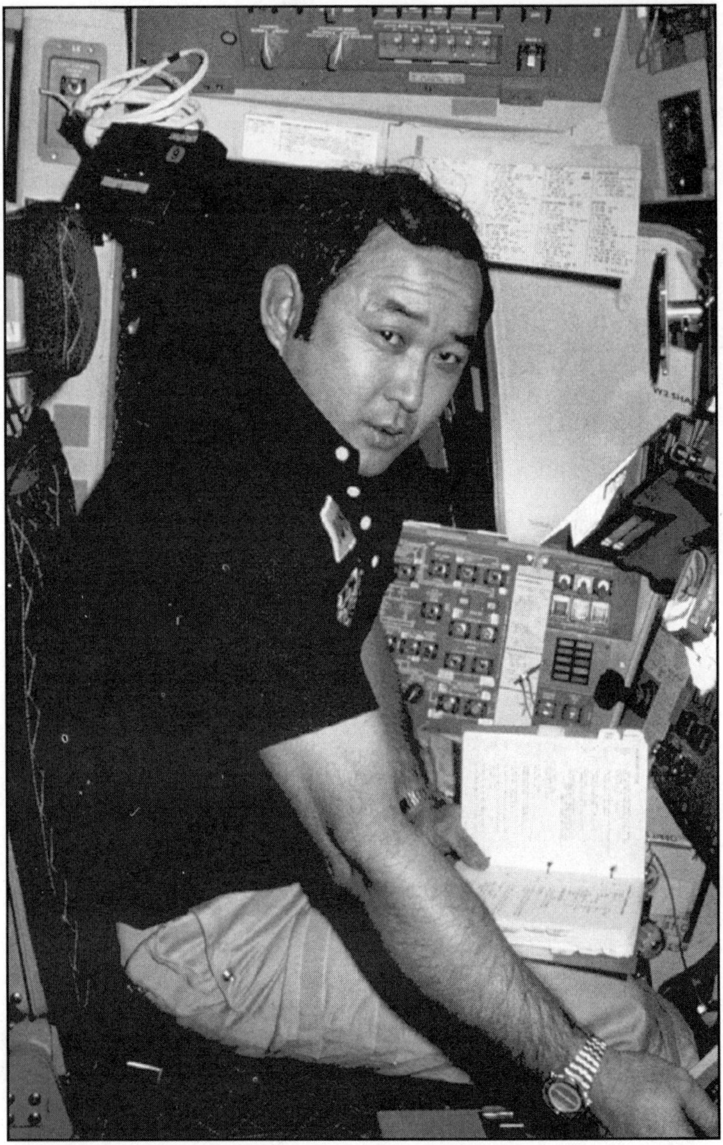

Ellison S. Onizuka realizes his lifelong dream of traveling in space. Here, he studies the flight checklist in preparation for his lauch aboard the space shuttle *Discovery*.

most happy, mostly because Onizuka was away so much of the time. One exception, however, was the Hawaiian luau that Onizuka hosted each year. The highlight of the event was a pig that was roasted in a deep pit that Onizuka built himself. In the weeks before the luau, Onizuka spent more time at home preparing for the event. He attended to every detail, including chopping down the required leaves from a swamp outside the base.

While El Onizuka was instructing air force officers and preparing roasted pigs, the National Aeronautics and Space Administration (NASA) was preparing to launch a new program. The first astronauts had explored new territory. The new astronauts would develop new technologies in areas such as weather forecasting, medicine, or communications that could be put to use on Earth. The first astronauts had been recruited as pilots. The new astronauts would not necessarily have to be pilots. Some would work as scientists in space. They would function in a new spaceship, called the shuttle because it could be used over and over again like a shuttle bus. The shuttle would be launched like a rocket and land like a plane. Previous U.S. space shots had dropped the astronauts in the ocean. This new venture was to be known as the Space Shuttle program.

NASA actively began to recruit women, African Americans, and other minorities for the space-shuttle missions. As Onizuka later commented, it didn't hurt him any to be an Asian American at that time! Unknown to his wife, he applied for astronaut training. Onizuka was pursuing the final leg of his childhood dream.

With NASA's encouragement, applications for astronauts skyrocketed in 1977. Of the 8,000 applications from that recruitment call, more than 1,600 were from women and more than 1,000 from other minorities. NASA chose 35 candidates to become the first space-shuttle astronauts. They included 24 white males, six women, three African Americans, one Native American, and one Asian American. One of the white males was Francis R. Scobee, who died in the crash of the *Challenger* shuttle in 1986. Of the six women, Sally Ride became the first U.S. woman astronaut in 1983, and Judith Resnick died in the *Challenger*. Of the three African Americans, Guion Bluford was the first to travel in space in 1983, Frederick Gregory became NASA's first African American pilot, and Ron McNair lost his life in the *Challenger* disaster. The Asian American, of course, was Ellison S. Onizuka.

Now a U.S. Air Force major, Onizuka was chosen as a finalist for the shuttle program. He was told to report to the space center in Houston to undergo a battery of tests. His wife—who by now had learned that he had applied for training—said that he was typically close mouthed about his chances of getting in. "There are so many qualified people," he said.

Despite the competition and uncertainty surrounding his selection, Onizuka worked hard to be in the best shape of his life before going to Houston. He lost weight,

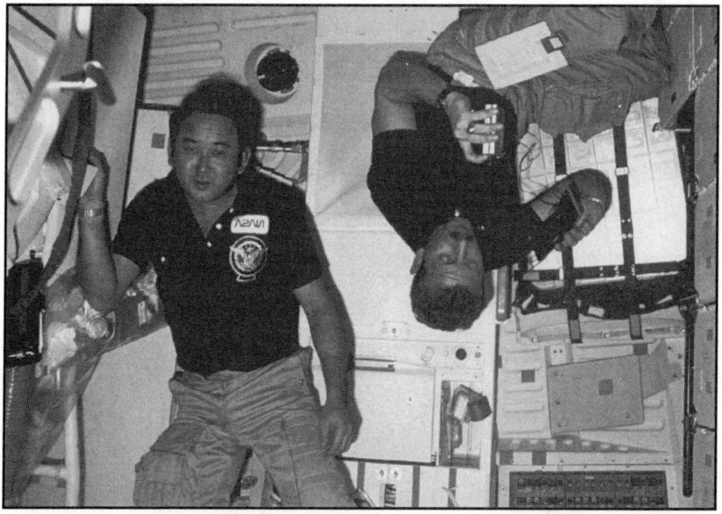

Mission specialist Ellison S. Onizuka "stands on the ceiling" in a 180-degree turn during weightlessness training. Pilot Loren J. Shriver (seated) records mission notes to command center, Houston.

ran daily, and did everything he could to stay in shape.

On January 16, 1978, Onizuka received a welcomed call. He had been selected for astronaut training. Delighted as he was, he accepted the news in a quiet way. When his wife told him that she was terrified about his venture into space, he said softly, "Everything is a risk." His family back in Hawaii was astounded when they heard the news. No one could picture "gentle El" flying around the Earth. Even after all his talk about airplanes, "it never dawned on me that he would become an astronaut," his brother Claude said.

There was no stopping Ellison Onizuka now. If life was hectic for the family before, it was nothing compared to life after they moved to Houston. Onizuka was in training and under evaluation at the Lyndon B. Johnson Space Center from early 1978 until August 1979. During that period, he often worked a 70-hour week. If certified for flight, he would be expected to act as a troubleshooter. That meant fixing just about anything on the shuttle that broke down. It also meant being prepared to walk in space if outside repairs were needed. His few free hours were spent with his family, and he developed a strong bond with his young daughters. He taught the girls how to plant a vegetable garden, and when he was home on Saturdays, he took young Janelle to feed the ducks.

Busy as he was, Onizuka hung on to his sense of humor. "It's hard not to laugh when you're standing on the ceiling," he said, referring to weightlessness-in-space training. He also vowed that he'd be the first to eat sushi, a Japanese dish of raw fish, in space.

Finally, Onizuka got the news he had been waiting for all his life. He had qualified for a space mission! He was going into space! One of the first things he did was to write a letter to his former scout leader back in Hawaii. "Getting to this point in my career," he said, "was an effort on the part of many people who have had an influence in my life. . . . It is only because of such people that others like me can grow up in the coffee fields of Kona and fly on the space shuttle."

Lieutenant Colonel Onizuka's first mission was aboard the space shuttle *Discovery*. His main job as mission specialist was to deploy a "spy" satellite for the Pentagon with the use of the shuttle's 50-foot remote arm. This mission was the first for the Department of

Defense. Many of the details about the flight were kept top secret. Onizuka took his Buddhist medallion on the flight for "security." He and four other astronauts blasted into space from the Kennedy Space Center in Florida on January 24, 1985. After 48 Earth orbits, the crew returned to Kennedy on January 27, one day early because of predicted bad weather. Onizuka had spent 74 hours in space.

He said later he didn't want to come down. "I still have to pinch myself that the dream came true."

Back in Hawaii, his family had all gathered at the Onizuka store for the launch. It was the first time the store had been closed for so long a period—10 days.

The Japanese American community went wild after Onizuka's flight. In Hawaii, they called him the "Lindbergh of the Big Island." This recalled Charles "Lucky Lindy" Lindbergh (1902-1974), one of America's greatest aviation heroes, who made the first solo, nonstop, transatlantic flight from New York to Paris in May 1927.

Onizuka, his wife, and his daughters went back to Hawaii as often as they could. He was toasted at lunches and dinners. He marched in parades, talked to children in classrooms, and gave speeches throughout the United States. He often talked about the "ride of a lifetime." He showed his pride in the space program by saying that "It's second to none," although he acknowledged that "There is still a long way to go." Through it all, Onizuka remained cheerful and humble. On one trip, he built a frame to hold the family mailbox on the side of the road. His mother said that like everything else he tackled, he did a good job. "It's going to last a long time," she said.

Onizuka's space career also looked like it was going to last a long while. Within a year of his first flight, he was selected for his second space mission. Onizuka was excited. He was to be a part of the seven-member space crew on flight STS-51L, aboard the *Challenger*. This was surely the most highly publicized and eagerly awaited space launch in U.S. history. It was dubbed the "all-American crew," showing off the United States and the NASA space program in all its racial and ethnic diversity. The commander was Air Force Major (Retired) Francis R. Scobee, 46, who, like Onizuka, was on his second space flight. The pilot was Navy Commander Michael J. Smith, 40, on his first flight. There were three mission specialists in charge of scientific experiments, all on their second flights. Besides Onizuka, there was Judith Resnick, 36, the second American woman in space, and Ronald McNair, 35, America's second African American astronaut. In addition, two civilians were going up for the first time. Gregory B. Jarvis, 41, was an electrical engineer, and Christa McAuliffe, 37, was a school teacher from New Hampshire.

It was all-American perfect—seven astronauts, two women, an African American, a Japanese American, and a school teacher!

Shortly before the scheduled launch, Onizuka spoke

An excited Ellison Onizuka and Christa McAuliffe smile with onlookers as they board the NASA bus that would take them to the space shuttle *Challenger*. Seventy-three seconds into its flight, the *Challenger* exploded, killing everyone on board.

to reporters at a press conference in what now seems almost like a premonition of disaster. He was asked if he thought it a good idea to have civilians, such as Christa McAuliffe, as part of the shuttle crew.

Always serious about space, Onizuka replied, "I personally don't feel that we should consider space flight routine. There's still a lot of questions about the shuttle. We should make sure it's safe as possible before we start flying too many civilians. However, I wouldn't mind a malfunction or two once the *Challenger* reaches orbit. We spent a lot of hours underwater training for an emergency space walk, and I'm anxious to try one."

A startled reporter asked if Onizuka really meant that he wanted something to go wrong.

The astronaut joked in reply, "I'd love to shinny up that remote manipulator arm. Be like shinnying up a coconut tree back home." There was a lot of laughter.

The night before Onizuka had to leave Houston for the space center in Florida, he went to his daughter's soccer game in Dallas. Lorna Onizuka said they didn't talk much about the upcoming flight because she was so nervous about it. Once he got to Florida, he called her to say that he had forgotten to bring his University of Colorado class ring with him. He regarded it a good-luck charm. Lorna promised to bring it when she arrived in Florida before the launch.

The *Challenger* was scheduled to blast off on January 23, 1986. But the weather didn't cooperate, so the flight was canceled. On Tuesday morning, January 28, the weather looked promising, except that it was cold—in fact, very cold for Florida.

There was some talk among NASA officials about danger from icicles breaking off the shuttle during liftoff. Could they somehow damage the incredibly tough-but-thin skin of the spacecraft? Should they go? Not go?

The decision was finally made. It would be okay. The mission was "go."

At 11:38 on the morning of January 28, 1986, the silver *Challenger* blasted off the launch pad in a great roar of noise and huge billows of smoke. Friends and family members of all the astronauts covered their ears to block out the deafening noise.

The *Challenger* streaked into the morning sun, climbing higher and faster. Ellison Onizuka was on his second "ride of a lifetime." At about 10,500 meters up (35,000 feet), the shuttle groaned and shuddered through some of the strongest winds ever encountered during a launch.

About a minute into the flight, ground control ordered "go at throttle up." This told flight commander Scobee to give the engines full power to get them into orbit. Scobee answered ground control with "Roger. Go at throttle up."

Then came the last sound recorded from a *Challenger* crew member. Pilot Smith was heard to say, "Uhh . . . oh!"

No one knows for sure what Smith saw, but in the next instant, the *Challenger* just blew up. It exploded into a giant fireball, engulfing the shuttle and plunging all seven crew members to their death in the Atlantic Ocean. Investigations later concluded that the cold temperature had caused the rubber seals on the shuttle to fail, causing the explosion.

It would be two years before the rings were redesigned and the space shuttle program was back in operation. The government agreed to cash settlements paid to the families of the *Challenger* astronauts. Lorna Onizuka remained in Houston to raise her daughters, who are now grown. Onizuka's mother remained in Hawaii until her death in 1990.

Ellison Onizuka served his country superbly and did his job well. He had found his dream, but it was all too short and certainly all too tragic. Yet, he knew the risks when he made plans for his career, and he was filling to face them. Courageous, fun loving, methodical, Onizuka lived by his personal code: "If you can't do it well, don't do it at all."

***

Ellison S. Onizuka

Career Highlights

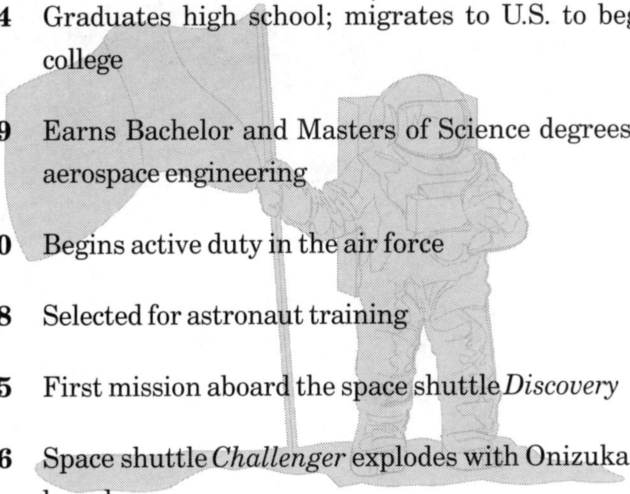

1964 Graduates high school; migrates to U.S. to begin college

1969 Earns Bachelor and Masters of Science degrees in aerospace engineering

1970 Begins active duty in the air force

1978 Selected for astronaut training

1985 First mission aboard the space shuttle *Discovery*

1986 Space shuttle *Challenger* explodes with Onizuka on board

Mae C. Jemison,
born 1956, says,

"

Don't be limited by others' limited imaginations.

"

MAE C. JEMISON

First African American Woman in Space

born 1956

She is a medical doctor and an engineer, a former Peace Corps officer and an astronaut. She loves to dance and play football. She has worked in poverty-stricken countries of West Africa as well as miles high in space. She has a cat named Sneeze. She is passionate about science but thinks that a person must be well rounded and interested in other things as well. She lives by these words: "Don't be limited by others' limited imaginations."

She is Dr. Mae C. Jemison, a slim package of unbelievable energy and the first African American woman in space. She says that she always knew she'd get there one day. She just didn't know how. Yet, even to her, the dream must have seemed very far away indeed. The National Aeronautics and Space Administration (NASA) was looking for astronauts who were everything Mae Jemison was not: a military jet pilot, a male, and white. Yet, she kept on dreaming. Perhaps she just refused to be limited by NASA's limited imagination at the time.

Born in Decatur, Alabama, on October 17, 1956, Mae Carol Jemison grew up in Chicago, which she calls her hometown. Her father, Charlie, worked as a carpenter, and her mother, Dorothy, was an elementary schoolteacher. Mae was the youngest of three. Her sister, Ada Jemison Bullock, is a child psychiatrist. Her brother, Charles, is a real-estate broker.

After being chosen for the space program, Jemison said, "I always assumed I would go into space ever since I was a little girl. I would have applied to be an astronaut if there had never been a single person going into space." Yet, when she entered Morgan Park High School in Chicago, her goals were a little more practical. Always fascinated with science, by her senior year she had decided on a career in biomedical engineering. The multitalented teenager was interested in many other pursuits as well, including art, anthropology, and the pompom squad.

The Jemison home was lower middle class. What the family lacked financially didn't come close to the strong family ties and the high value the family placed on their African heritage. Peggy Jackson-Chase, speech and drama teacher at Morgan High, knows Mae Jemison well. "The school was sixty-forty white, and Mae was very conscious of her African American heritage. But she got along well with white kids too, and when the United Students Group was formed to combat problems in the school, Mae was active in that," she said.

Peggy Jackson-Chase is also the faculty advisor for the Morgan High School paper, called the *Empehi News*, which frequently features stories about their famous graduate. The teacher added, "Mae was popular. She was

A childhood fascination with science led astronaut Mae C. Jemison to break NASA's white, all-male, jet piolt standards for the space program. Jemison (center) conducts emergency procedures during training.

a leader, and you can't lead if you're not popular. In fact, she was very well liked and a wonderful student. Though math and science were her primary interests, she was active in the Modern Dance Club, the African American Club, the student council, and drama. The neighborhood around Morgan High was friendly and safe, but Mae went to school right after the King assassination, and there were problems within the school and in Chicago as a whole resulting from that."

Religious and civil-rights leader Martin Luther King, Jr., was assassinated near Memphis, Tennessee, in 1968. His death sparked racial tension throughout the country, especially in large urban areas with a high concentration of African Americans and whites who were living together under cramped city conditions.

King had led the Montgomery, Alabama, bus boycott in 1956. The boycott started the movement toward desegregation in the South. In 1963, before a crowd of some 200,000 in Washington, D.C., he gave his famous "I have a dream" speech in which he envisioned freedom and justice for all races. His white assassin, James Earl Ray, was sentenced to 99 years in prison.

Jemison graduated from Morgan High in 1973. She was just 16 years old when she entered Stanford University in California on a National Achievement Scholarship. Her academic record and extracurricular activities roster at Stanford are even harder to believe than her high school accomplishments. Besides double-majoring in chemical engineering and African and African American studies, she was the first female head of the all-black student union. Among other things, Jemison was involved in intramural football and dance and theater productions. Jemison explains her interests this way, "One's love for science doesn't get rid of all the other areas. Someone interested in science should be interested in understanding what's going on in the world. That means you have to find out about social science, art, and politics."

Jemison didn't forget about space. The dream was still there. During her senior year at Stanford, NASA began a new recruitment program for the space shuttle. Minorities and women were encouraged to apply.

Surprisingly, Mae Jemison did not apply. Jemison wanted to pursue her space career when it was the right time for her. In 1977, she took her Bachelor of Science degree in chemical engineering and headed to Cornell University Medical College in New York City. She had also earned a Bachelor of Arts degree in African and African American studies.

As though working for a medical degree didn't take up enough time, Jemison served as president of both the Cornell Medical Student Executive Council and the National Student Medical Association. She traveled in Cuba, worked in Thailand at a refugee camp, and spent some time in Kenya with the African Medical and Research Foundation. "It's interesting to see different ways of living," she said.

Jemison earned her medical degree from Cornell in 1981. She completed her internship at the Los Angeles County/University of Southern California Medical Center in 1982. By July of that year, she was in private practice in Los Angeles, but—not for long.

Never one to stay put, Dr. Jemison joined the Peace Corps in January 1983. She spent the next two-and-a-half years in West Africa administering health-care programs. She felt that the experience was good for her because, as one of the youngest doctors there, she had to assert herself as a physician.

Jemison returned to Los Angeles in 1985 and worked as a general practitioner at CIGNA Health Plans of California. That left her evenings free, so she took engineering courses at UCLA. Just when it looked as though her medical career was finally about to settle down, that old dream popped up again. Perhaps it was just that she'd already done about everything she had set out to do and had been about anywhere she wanted to go. What was there left to see but space?

Mae Jemison applied to NASA for entrance in the astronaut program in October 1985. This time, the time was right for her.

Unfortunately, the time wasn't right for NASA. In January 1986, the shuttle *Challenger* blew up, plunging the U.S. space program into an uncertain future. It took until the end of the year for NASA once again to call for astronaut candidates. Jemison reapplied.

In February 1987, Jemison was called from Houston, Texas. She was one of 15 chosen for astronaut training out of 2,000 applicants. She remembers that when she heard the news, it took her a while to stop smiling. Her teenage dream was about to come true. She was already an engineer and a doctor. She'd been a Peace Corps officer overseas and a general practitioner. Oh yes, she also spoke Swahili, Japanese, and Russian. Now she was going into space. She was just 30 years old.

If Mae Carol Jemison's accomplishments seem almost too good to be true, believe it. As the saying goes, "You can't make this stuff up."

Normally low-keyed, Jemison was suddenly thrust into the spotlight. Not only was she one of the few chosen for space training, but she was also the first African American woman chosen for space training. A little uncomfortable with the role-model status, she said, "The

The Peace Corps was created in 1961 by President John F. Kennedy. His brother-in-law, R. Sargent Shriver, was its first director. The idea was for volunteer Americans to assist people in other countries by working in such fields as education, trade, and agriculture. Volunteers are expected to work in the host country for about two years. Today, there are some 5,000 Peace Corps volunteers in about 90 countries.

thing that I have done throughout my life is to do the best job that I can and to be me. . . . I'd like to be someone who says, 'No, don't try necessarily to be like me or live your life or grow up to be an astronaut or a physician unless that's what you want to do.'"

Now began what was Jemison's longest stay in one place since high school. From 1987 until 1992, she trained out of the Lyndon B. Johnson Space Center in Houston, Texas. To be selected for the space program, a candidate must be between 5 feet and 6 feet 4 inches tall, must have eyesight correctable to 20/20, and must have fairly low blood pressure. Jemison met all those criteria, being slim and 5 feet 9 inches tall. During the first year of basic training, astronaut candidates become familiar with the space shuttle and the hardware that they will be working with in space. They also find out such simple but important facts as whether or not they get airsick or suffer from claustrophobia (a fear of closed-in spaces). That would never do for someone who plans to be shut up in a tiny capsule and blasted miles high into the sky. Fortunately, Jemison doesn't become airsick and doesn't suffer from that closed-in feeling. She also went through a water-survival course at Homestead Air Force Base in Florida, a parachute-survival course at Vance Air Force Base in Oklahoma, and a wilderness-survival course at Fairchild Air Force Base in Washington State. There, she learned how to find food in the wilderness and to make her own survival equipment from parachute gear. All these courses prepare astronauts for a possible emergency ejection.

Then, at long last, it was time. The crew was chosen for the upcoming flight of the space shuttle *Endeavour*. The mission would carry seven astronauts, among them the first African American woman, Dr. Mae C. Jemison.

In an awesome cloud of smoke and orange fire, the shuttle *Endeavour*, flight STS-47, blasted off from the Kennedy Space Center in Florida on September 12, 1992. It was dream come true for the girl from Chicago. But however high the excitement, probably no U.S. astronaut since 1986 ever blasted off into space without remembering the *Challenger* explosion.

"You're aware that you are sitting on a controlled explosion," Jemison said later. "But you also realize that you've taken all the precautions. You trust the people you have been working with, and you know that they have worked to try to keep things safe. After that, you have to leave it alone. If you keep worrying about it, then you're not going to be able to do your job."

Each astronaut on a space-shuttle mission has a specific job. The commander has onboard responsibility for the vehicle, the crew, and the safety of the flight. The pilot assists the commander in controlling and operating the shuttle. The rest of the shuttle crew is

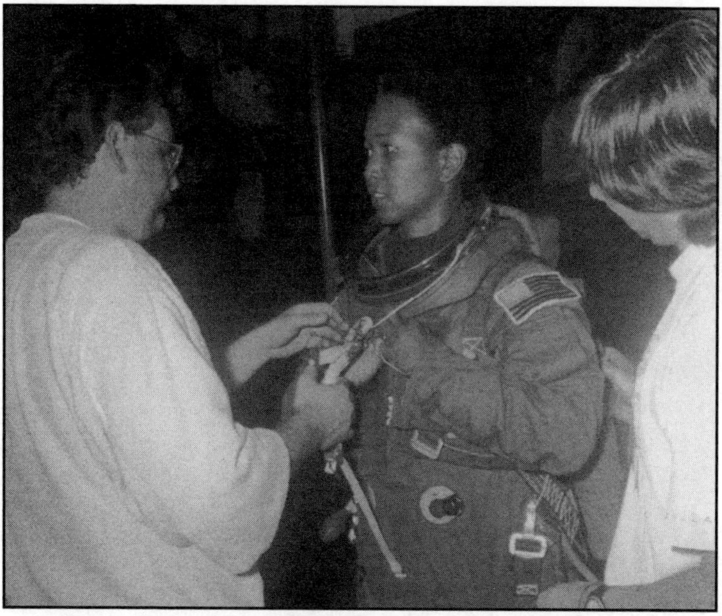

Dr. Mae C. Jemison, the first African American woman astronaut, gets help with her spacesuit for her first flight in space.

made up of mission specialists and, on some flights, a payload specialist.

The mission-specialist astronaut has overall responsibility for coordinating shuttle operations that concern shuttle systems and any planned experiments. It is the mission specialist who walks in space and executes maneuvers called EVAs (extravehicular activities). It is the mission specialist who also operates the remote manipulator system (RMS). This is the long robot arm that can pluck a nonfunctioning satellite out of space and bring it back to the shuttle for repair or for the trip home. Finally the mission specialist is responsible for specific experiments planned for particular flights.

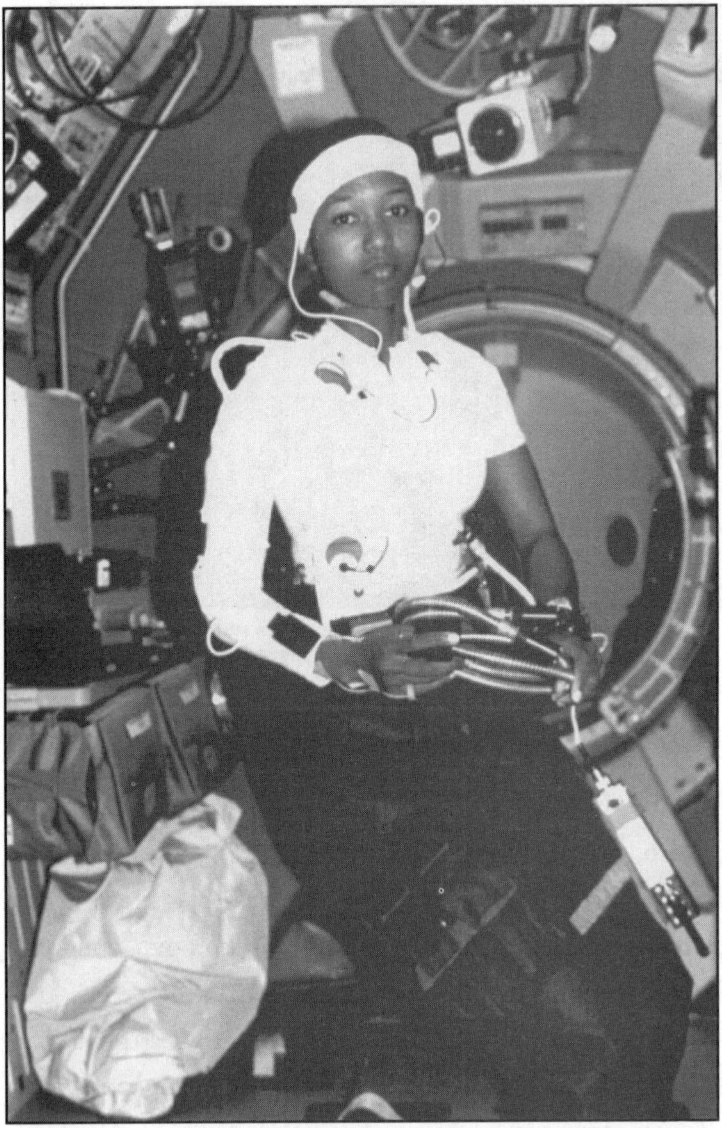

Dr. Mae C.Jemison, a science mission specialist on the *Endeavour*, performs an experiment to study the effects of weightlessness on the development of frog eggs fertilized in space.

The payload specialist is not a NASA astronaut. He or she may be a citizen of a foreign country that is sending up a communications satellite, for instance, via the space shuttle. The payload specialist might also be a U.S. citizen who is connected with a particular business or government branch. The *Challenger* flight, for example, had carried two payload specialists. One of them was Gregory B. Jarvis, an engineer for the Hughes Aircraft Company. The other was Christa McAuliffe, a New Hampshire schoolteacher who was chosen to be the first private citizen in space.

Jemison was a mission specialist on the *Endeavour*. During the eight-day flight, she conducted experiments that dealt with weightlessness and the use of biofeedback techniques to ease motion sickness in space. This was especially important because many astronauts, unlike Jemison, suffer from motion sickness in flight. She also tested how much calcium human bones lose in space. This is important because a loss of calcium can weaken bones and cause them to break easily.

After more than 190 hours orbiting the Earth, Jemison and the *Endeavour* made a successful return. The first African American female astronaut said that she hoped that her flight would encourage both women and minority members to think of space as a challenge and a career. "My participation in the space-shuttle mission," she said, "helps to say that all peoples of the world have astronomers, physicists, and explorers." Jemison, who is a passionate advocate of women's

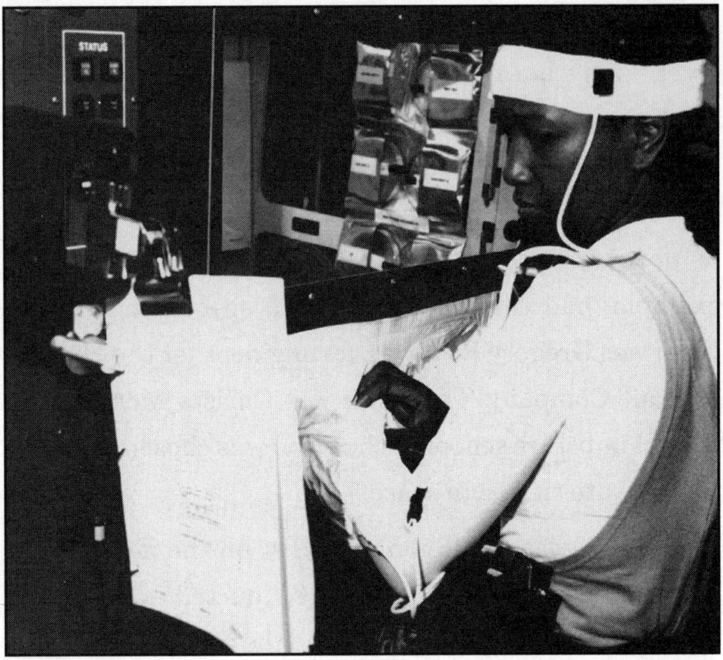

Dr. Jemison, a physician and astronaut, wears a headband and other monitoring gear at various times to test biofeedback techniques in space.

rights, also said, "More women should demand to be involved in the space program. This is one area where we can get in on the ground floor and possibly help to direct where space exploration will go in the future."

Since her historic flight, Jemison has received many honors, including honorary doctorates, the Ebony Black Achievement Award in 1992, and a Montgomery Fellowship from Dartmouth College in 1993. She was named the Gamma Sigma Gamma Woman of the Year in 1989, and in 1992, an alternative public school was dedicated to her in Detroit, Michigan. The principal, S. Hopkins, explains, "The Mae C. Jemison Academy is a public school emphasizing math and science. Children are admitted by the lottery system after indicating that they wish to enroll in the academy. Classes include preschool through the fourth grade and are centered on African ethnic studies.

"Mae Jemison comes to the school once a year," said Principal Hopkins. "When she does, she actually teaches classes. Through the year, she sends materials and reading matter with funds from various foundations with which she is involved. She is very much concerned with the future of the children, and she always delivers this message: 'Hold tight to your dreams, and do the best you can.'"

Will Jemison continue to be a role model? "That's for other people to decide," she says. "I do think that I serve as an important image for society in general—certainly for young black girls who need to see themselves represented in all areas, but just as much for older white males who make decisions many times as to who will be allowed to develop talents and be given opportunities to excel."

Certainly Mae Jemison has developed her talents and taken advantage of her given opportunities to excel. After she left NASA in 1993, Jemison, who lives in Houston, began her own company. She is the president of the Jemison Group, which researches, develops, and markets advanced technologies. One of its projects is a space-based telecommunication system that should speed up health-care delivery to developing world countries.

Where will this dynamo doctor-engineer-astronaut-businesswoman go in the future? Is the space dream over? No way, declares Jemison, who also plans to continue the practice of medicine. In an interview not long ago, she declared that she would go to another planet at the drop of a hat. Mars, anyone?

***

Mae C. Jemison
Career Highlights

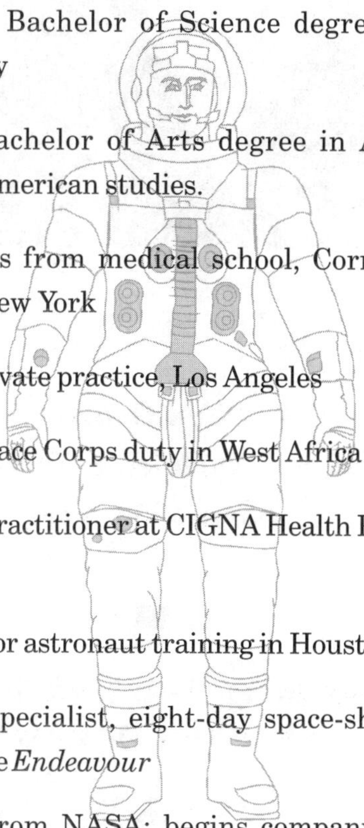

1977 Receives Bachelor of Science degree, Stanford University

Earns Bachelor of Arts degree in African and African American studies.

1981 Graduates from medical school, Cornell Medical Center, New York

1982 Opens private practice, Los Angeles

1983 Begins Peace Corps duty in West Africa

1985 General practitioner at CIGNA Health Plans, Los Angeles

1987 Selected for astronaut training in Houston

1992 Mission specialist, eight-day space-shuttle flight aboard the *Endeavour*

1993 Resigns from NASA; begins company called the Jemison Group

Ellen Ochoa
First Hispanic American Woman in Space, born 1958, says

"

You should not be afraid to dream of something very high.

"

ELLEN OCHOA

First Hispanic American Woman in Space

born 1958

On November 14, 1994, dragging a huge parachute behind it, the space shuttle *Atlantis* touched down on the hard, flat surface of the Mojave Desert near Edwards Air Force Base in California. The landing was perfect even though it had been scheduled for Cape Canaveral, Florida. Bad weather caused by tropical storm Gordon had diverted the landing to the West Coast. Of the seven shuttle flights launched by the National Aeronautics and Space Administration (NASA) in 1994, four of them had landed in California's Mojave Desert because of bad weather in Florida. NASA avoids landing shuttle flights in California, if possible, because it costs $1 million to get the space shuttle back to the launch site at Cape Canaveral! The shuttle must travel piggyback on a jumbo jet.

From the November mission, the *Atlantis* brought home 10 rats, a shuttleload of data on atmospheric research, and six astronauts. One of the astronauts was 36-year-old Ellen Ochoa, the first Hispanic American woman in space.

Even though the November mission was Ochoa's second flight in space, it still seemed like an impossible dream come true. Back in 1993, before her first shuttle flight, she spoke to highschool students in her hometown of La Mesa, California. She told them to keep on dreaming. She told them how much things had changed for people who dreamed of a career in space in the years since she had been a student.

"When I was young and I was watching Mercury and Apollo astronauts, they were all men," she said. "They were all generally in the military. There were a few scientists who were chosen, but not a large number, so it didn't seem like something that you could dream to grow up and be. But now it's very different. It's open to anybody. You just need to study math and science in school."

A scientist herself, Dr. Ochoa told the students, "You should not be afraid to dream of something very high. Certainly, when I first watched the astronauts going into space and thought about becoming an astronaut myself, it seemed like an impossible dream. But a lot of hard work and a little bit of luck can make something like that come true."

The dream certainly came true for Ellen Ochoa. She was born in Los Angeles, California, on May 10, 1958, but grew up in La Mesa as the third of five children. Her parents divorced when Ellen was 12. Her father, who was Mexican, was not a part of her life thereafter. She was raised by her mother, who is an American of German-English-Scottish heritage.

Ellen's mother, Rosanne Ochoa, said that her daughter was "an easy child to raise. She had a great

For as long as there have been humans, there seems to have been rats. They can survive just about anywhere in the world, including space! These aggressive, active, and adaptable creatures have highly developed senses and breed easily. They also transmit diseases easily. For centuries, humans have been trying to get rid of rats or at least to control them, with varying degrees of success. Although rats in general do not rate high with the public, they are a favorite laboratory animal for tests, and that includes out in space.

sense of humor and was fun to be with. She liked school, she worked summers, she studied hard, and enjoyed music. In fact, she made it easier to be a parent."

The Ochoas remain a close and loving family, although today they are somewhat scattered around the country. Rosanne Ochoa feels that their closeness is partly due to her decision to remain in the same house after the divorce and to try to keep things as normal as possible. With financial support from her ex-husband, she was able to stay at home until the children were grown. The two oldest are Beth, a law-school student, and Monte, a multimedia specialist with the San Diego school system. The two youngest are Tyler, an attorney teaching law at Whittier College in California, and Wilson, who plays the French horn with the Charleston (North Carolina) symphony orchestra. The middle child, Ellen, occasionally flies off into space.

Asked how her parent's divorce affected her childhood, Ellen Ochoa said, "I was more determined to have a career where I wouldn't need to depend on anyone." She added, "For me, education was the key to getting an interesting and exciting job. Do well in school and get an education, and anything is possible. That's certainly what worked for me." Ochoa also says that her mother has been the greatest influence in her life. "She was the one who encouraged everyone in the family to get a good education," she said, and they did. All five of the Ochoa children were honor students, and Ellen, Tyler, and Wilson were valedictorians in their senior years at Grossmont High School.

After Grossmont, Ochoa enrolled at San Diego State University. She graduated in 1980—as class covaledictorian—with a bachelor's degree in physics and a grade point average of 4.0. But, as she readily points out when she talks to students, it may take some time for a person to find his or her special talent, to learn where he or she really wants to go. "I didn't really get into science until San Diego State," she said, "and I really didn't decide on a career until graduate school." In fact, Ochoa changed her major *five* times before settling on physics! Once the final decision was made, however, she really buckled down. In fact,

At age 13, Ellen Ochoa studied hard and dreamed the impossible: a career in space.

Ellen Ochoa, shown here in her senior year in Grossmont High School, was the first of three valedictorians in the school.

her senior lab thesis in Physics 553 was so good that it is now a standard experiment conducted by everyone who takes the class.

Stanford University was the next stop on the way to space. By 1985, she had earned a doctorate in electrical engineering. Her Ph.D. thesis resulted in a U.S. patent.

She is also listed as co-inventor on two patents obtained when she worked at Sandia National Laboratories in Livermore, California. She had joined Sandia's research staff after graduation. Optics, which deals with the origin and extension of light, was now her special interest.

In 1988, Ochoa went to the NASA Ames Research Center, Moffett Field, California. There, she headed a research group that worked primarily on optical systems for space. Her next assignment was as chief of the Intelligent Systems Technology Branch, heading a group of 35 scientists and engineers who researched computer systems for space missions.

Perhaps the move closer to space as an Ames employee prompted Ochoa to apply for the space program. In fact, she had submitted an application to NASA after her graduation in 1985. "When I first thought about it, I thought there was absolutely no chance I would be selected." She was right. She wasn't. The time seemed right again in 1987, and Ochoa reapplied. A total of 1,945 applicants made it through the first round. This narrowed down to 106 men and women who were called for an interview at the Lyndon B. Johnson Space Center in Houston.

Some interview! First, she had to undergo a week of tests at the space center to determine if she could handle the equipment that must be used in space. She could. Then, her 5-feet-5-inch, 108-pound frame was medically examined to decide if she was physically fit for the rigors of space travel. She was. Next, she endured an extensive review by the NASA astronaut selection board.

Apparently, Ellen Ochoa did okay on all her tests because she was selected, in January 1990, to begin training for NASA's astronaut program. She was one of 22, five of whom were women. She was also the first Hispanic American woman in the new group.

How was Ellen Ochoa chosen to become an astronaut? What does NASA look for?

Qualifications for astronaut training have changed greatly since the first U.S. manned space flight in 1961. The original astronauts were all white, all male, and all military pilots with some engineering training. They could be no more than 5 feet 11 inches tall. Otherwise, they wouldn't have fit into the tiny Mercury space capsule in use back in 1961. Today's space capsules are not exactly roomy, but they are larger than the Mercury type.

Of the original 500 candidates who applied when the space program began, NASA selected seven. Three were from the Navy: M. Scott Carpenter, Walter M. Schirra, Jr., and Alan B. Shepard, Jr., the first U.S. astronaut to go into space in 1961. One was a marine: John H. Glenn, Jr., the first U.S. astronaut to orbit the Earth (1962) and now a U.S. Senator from Ohio. Three were air force officers: L. Gordon Cooper, Jr.;

In the 1990 U.S. Census, Americans of Hispanic/Spanish descent made up 9 percent of the population. They account for about 22 million of the 248 million people in the United States.

Virgil "Gus" Grissom, who died in a spacecraft fire on the ground in 1967; and Donald K. "Deke" Slayton, the only one of the seven who did not fly in the original Mercury space program. He was grounded for medical reasons. Slayton finally made it into space in 1975 when he flew on the U.S.-Russian mission known as the Apollo-Soyuz Test Project.

When NASA began its space-shuttle program in the late 1970s, requirements had changed. The new astronauts no longer had to be white, or males, or military pilots. Women and minorities were actively recruited. They still had to meet certain qualifications. Whether applying as a pilot or a mission specialist, a candidate must have at least a bachelor's degree in engineering or a related field, plus a minimum of three years of professional experience. Besides being in excellent health, each must be between 64 and 76 inches tall to fit in the spacecraft.

After meeting these basic requirements, candidates must go through a week-long process of interviews and medical and psychological examinations. Because NASA must fill just a few jobs from so many applicants, personal interviews become very important. NASA looks for people who are independent enough to function in the unknown of space and cooperative enough to get along with other crew members in very tight working and living spaces.

Candidates for astronaut training have about a 20 percent chance of being selected. Those who are chosen spend a year at the Johnson Space Center in Houston, Texas, for training and evaluation. This training includes parachuting, land and water survival, and weightlessness experience.

At the year's end, final selection is made. If the astronaut selected is a civilian, he or she is expected to stay in the program for at least five years. If the astronaut is in the military, he or she is transferred to NASA for a specified tour of duty, depending on the project.

About 10 months before a flight, the astronauts begin to train for that particular mission. Together, the crew learns to work as a team in space. Nothing is overlooked, including emergency plans if something goes wrong. Even after the mission is completed and the crew is home, their training isn't over. They spend several days in medical testing and debriefing. Their experiences help to make the next shuttle flight safer and even more successful for its crew.

Ochoa successfully completed astronaut training and eagerly awaited her first space flight. That came on April 8, 1993, in a night launch of the shuttle *Discovery* from the Kennedy Space Center. Ochoa was the only rookie of the five-member crew. As a mission specialist in charge of experiments on board, she was responsible for operating the mechanical arm that releases and captures satellites in space. Ochoa successfully released a small satellite, called *Spartan*, to measure solar wind produced by the sun. Two days later, Ochoa used the

Payload commander astronaut Ellen Ochoa secures herself in a small life raft during an emergency training exercise at the Johnson Space Center, Houston.

mechanical arm to retrieve the satellite for *Discovery's* return to Earth on April 17.

Back home, a proud mother said of her daughter's achievements, "It doesn't surprise me." It didn't surprise Professor Joseph Goodman of Stanford University either. He described his star pupil in glowing terms: "She is a wonderful person and well organized.

Mission specialist Ellen Ochoa performs the Marine Corps Hymn, the Navy Hymn, and "God Save the Queen" for fellow crew members on *Discovery's* flight deck.

She's steady. You can count on her. When she went to NASA, she rose like a rocket. She's also an outstanding manager, and the fact that she's good with people helps to make her a good manager. She has a friendly personality and is a good communicator. Besides all that, she plays the flute! She even gave solo concerts at Stanford."

Another person who sings the praises of astronaut Ochoa is her father-in-law, Louis Zak of Waldport, Oregon. While working at the NASA Ames Research Center in California, Ochoa met Coe Fulmer Miles, an electrical engineer. In fact, she was his boss! They married and Coe decided to change his career. He is now attending law school in Houston, where the couple lives.

Father-in-law Zak, who is Coe's stepfather, said, "She's a people person. She's very outgoing and does many speaking engagements. She's always loved flying. In fact, she flies her own plane. We're very close to Ellen and Coe, but we're too far away. We're in Oregon and they're in Houston."

Ellen's husband, Coe, is not the only one in the family to change careers. When Rosanne Ochoa encouraged her children to work hard for success, those weren't just empty words. In 1982, 22 years after she took her first class at San Diego State, the elder Ochoa earned her bachelor of arts degree! "My first priority was raising the children, and school came second," she said.That's perseverance!

For her second space flight in 1994, Ellen Ochoa was

Ellen Ochoa has a passion for flying. When she's not working at NASA, she flies her own plane.

promoted to payload commander. That meant that she was in charge of the equipment and materials for the mission aboard the *Atlantis* in November. The main scientific emphasis this time was atmospheric research. Ochoa's job was to make sure that these experiments were carried out properly. Ochoa and the other crew members carried a $35 million German satellite as part of the ship's payload. The satellite was released on the second day of the flight and retrieved eight days later. *Atlantis* and crew returned to Earth on November 14, 1994. The experiments worked perfectly on the flight.

The crew of the *Atlantis* also experienced something else that was unique. The shuttle flew over the edges of the gaping ozone hole near the Antarctic. All living creatures on Earth are protected from ultraviolet radiation by a layer of oxygen that forms naturally in the upper atmosphere. This layer is called the ozone layer. Scientists have long warned that the chemicals that are manufactured on Earth are destroying the ozone layer. The flight of the *Atlantis* offered more proof of that warning.

What is next for astronaut Ellen Ochoa? As far as she is concerned, just more of the same. "I might want to be an astronaut for the rest of my life," she has said, and maybe she will. It seems certain that whatever she makes up her mind to do, she will follow through and do it successfully.

Ellen Ochoa truly believes that you can make your dreams come true if you work at it. When she speaks to students, she says, "Anyone can grow up to have an exciting career like this," and she means it. She encourages students to explore a career in space with a natural enthusiasm that is so much a part of her. Space, she reminds them, doesn't have to be blasting off in a shuttle. "There are very exciting jobs in the space program other than being an astronaut," she says. "There are scientists, engineers, designers, all sorts of things. It's realistic to think of space as a career."

But for Ellen Ochoa, the first Hispanic American woman astronaut, high in space, looking down on Earth is definitely where she plans to be for a long, long time.

***

Ellen Ochoa

Career Highlights

1980 Receives Bachelor of Science degree, San Diego State

1985 Graduates with Ph.D. in Electrical Engineering, Stanford University; applies and is turned down for space program

1988 Goes to work for NASA Ames Research Center, California

1990 Joins the space program

1993 April 8, first space flight, aboard *Discovery*

1994 November 11, second space flight, aboard *Atlantis*

Vocabulary

By the time students finish this book, they should know all the following vocabulary words. These words are related to values and were chosen to encourage students to explore and form their own values as they read and learn more about role models.

- achiever
- advantage
- advocate
- career
- challenge
- character
- competitive
- cooperative
- criteria
- dedicated
- defeat
- determined
- disciplined
- diversity
- education
- enthusiastic
- evaluation
- excel
- goals
- heritage
- honor student
- image
- independent
- leadership
- methodical
- minorities
- mission specialist
- nurture
- opportunities
- passionate
- patent
- pioneers
- positive
- premonition
- price
- qualifications
- racial barriers
- recruitment
- risk
- role model
- success
- talent
- team
- thesis
- triumph
- unassuming
- valedictorian
- values
- well-rounded
- women's rights

Vocabulary

ROBERT H. LAWRENCE, JR.

disciplined
achiever
qualifications
price
minorities
triumph
defeat
nurture
role model
recruitment

GUION S. BLUFORD, JR.

success
racial barriers
values
character
advantage
goals
leadership
dedicated
pioneers
opportunities

ELLISON S. ONIZUKA

determined
methodical
competitive
risk
unassuming
positive
enthusiastic
premonition
evaluation
diversity

MAE C. JEMISON

passionate
well-rounded
heritage
criteria
challenge
career
advocate
women's rights
image
excel

ELLEN OCHOA

education
honor student
talent
thesis
patent
valedictorian
mission specialist
independent
cooperative
team